### A MINI-POSTER BOOK

**COMPILATION**
CYNTHIA HART

**PHOTOGRAPHS**
JEFFREY E. BLACKMAN
AND
GEOFFREY BIDDLE

**TEXT**
LIONEL LIBSON

SCHOLASTIC INC.

# GLOSSARY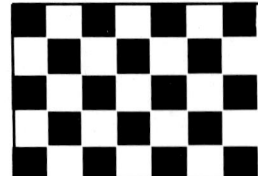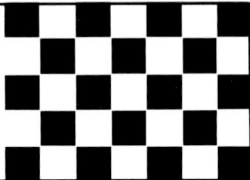

**BMX:** Bicycle motocross.
**Berm:** A banked bend in a racing track.
**Cranking:** Pedaling very hard.
**Freestyling:** Stunt riding, as opposed to racing.
**Getting air:** Defying gravity. Taking off a ramp or quarterpipe for maximum climb.
**Gnarly:** Hard, difficult.
**Moto:** A race, or heat.
**Rad:** (radical) Fearless, off-the-wall. Taking a trick as far as you and your bike can go.
**Serious:** Difficult or skilled.
**Speedjumping:** A racing technique for going through a jump as fast and low to the ground as possible. Wheelie before the jump, continue pedaling, and shift weight to the rear wheel.
**Tabletop:** A freestyling trick in which the rider takes the bike high into the air, turning the bike frame flat or parallel to the ground at the top of the jump. Also, a raised flat obstacle in a BMX track.
**Wheelie:** Riding on one wheel. Used in BMX racing to set up speedjumps.
**Whoop-de-doo:** Closely spaced mounds in a BMX track.
**Wired:** In control. Knowing a trick or technique well enough to do it right, again and again.

BMX bicycle riding involves a high degree of physical risk. This book is not in any way intended to be an instructional book on BMX. Proper instruction, training, and safety equipment should be obtained before anyone participates in this sport.

With special thanks to Ben Prentiss, Todd Williams, and Eric Liebowitz

No part of this publication may be reproduced in whole or in part, or stored in a retrieval system, or transmitted in any form or by any means, electronic, mechanical, photocopying, recording, or otherwise, without written permission of the publisher. For information regarding permission, write to Scholastic Inc., 730 Broadway, New York NY 10003.

ISBN 0-590-40577-2

Compilation copyright © 1984 by Cynthia Hart.
Cover photo © Geoffrey Biddle
All rights reserved. Published by Scholastic Inc.

12 11 10 9 8 7 6 5 4

Printed in the U.S.A.

9/8 0 1/9

Geoffrey Biddle

BMX means bicycle motocross. The sport was invented in California during the late sixties by a few boys who tried racing their bicycles on a motorcyle cross country track. Since then, BMX has grown, and there are now BMX tracks, clubs, and teams across the country and around the world.

© Geoffrey Biddle

There are two basic forms of BMX: racing on a special dirt track, and freestyle trick-riding. This ultra-rad freestyler tries for maximum hang time with intricate twists while frozen in midair. You practice tricks the way you practice racing—over and over 'til you've got it wired.

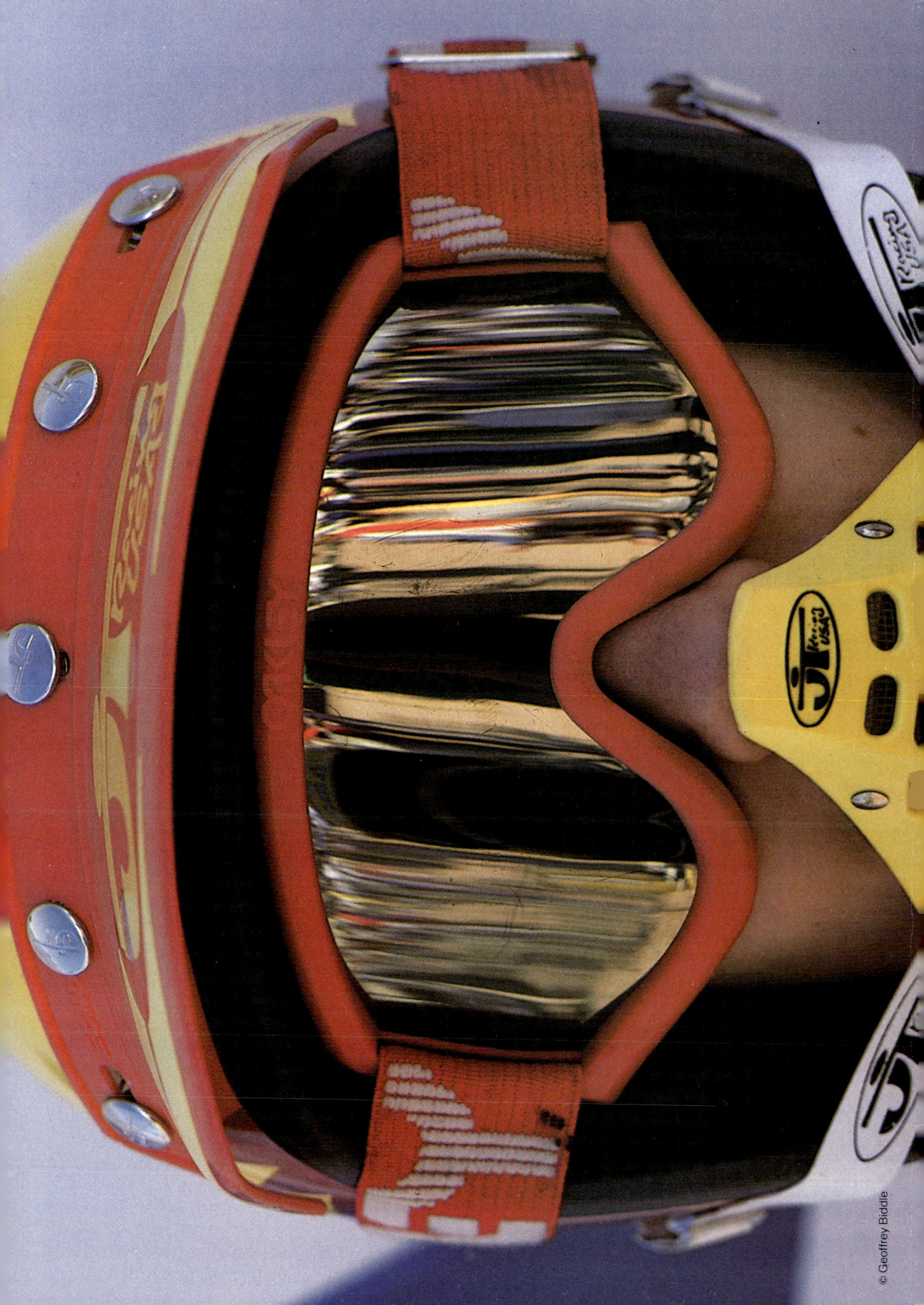

© Geoffrey Biddle

Super-psyched? Only the man behind the mask knows, before things get really radical. The high-impact helmet takes much of the danger out of spills. Visors and face masks give added protection. Additional touches such as "all business" decals say a lot about the rider and can make a helmet a personal statement.

Keep cool. Try to remember everything you learned about the course during practice because things move really fast at race time. Since new motos start as soon as the previous ones finish, riders line up behind the starting line so they will be ready when their turn comes. BMX bikers range in age from 6 to 17 and over. Most riders are between 10 and 16.

© Geoffrey Biddle

Grab that inside line on the turn. Lean in hard and keep more weight on the front tire. The extended leg helps your balance on a tight curve and can make the rider behind you go a little slower or wider. Since a moto lasts only about 40 seconds, fine-tuned riding skills are essential to winning.

© Jeffrey E. Blackman

Whoop-de-doos turn BMX mean machines into buckin' broncs. Whoop-de-doos are three or four humps built close together in the track to make a corrugated effect. The best way to handle them in a race is to go as fast as possible *without* jumping.

Bumps and spills. You don't learn to win without taking a few. Pads over the top bar of the frame, across the handlebars, and over the stem of the bike, give vital protection. A helmet, long sleeves, and long pants are also important to cut down on injuries.

© Geoffrey Biddle

Getting dressed on the family car is a good way to keep an eye on the competition. Your racing gear, from helmet to jersey, is important. When you're lookin' good you'll be ridin' good. Many riders on the BMX circuit travel long distances to get to a race. Mom, Dad, brothers and sisters–they all help, because BMX is a family team effort.

© Geoffrey Biddle

The small, rugged, 20-inch-wheel BMX bicycle evolved from the Stingray-style bike. Your bike can be bought ready-made or built from scratch. From brakes to crank, from chain to crossbar, every part can be an important choice. The frame and forks are the key to BMX success. The best are built from chrome-moly or chrome-alloy steel. Tubes are joined with TIG welding—a method that looks like icing on a birthday cake.

Getting dressed on the family car is a good way to keep an eye on the competition. Your racing gear, from helmet to jersey, is important. When you're lookin' good you'll be ridin' good. Many riders on the BMX circuit travel long distances to get to a race. Mom, Dad, brothers and sisters–they all help, because BMX is a family team effort.

Winning isn't the only thing in BMX, but it's a lot. This trophy garden tells us we're looking at a heavy-duty racer, and Scott Frey has been a big winner, seeing a lot of BMX action in a short time.

© Geoffrey Biddle

Two of BMX's all-time winners, Stu Thomsen (left) and Greg Hill, rest between races during 1983 competition. Some riders stay amateurs, but the best often turn professional and ride for money. Factory sponsorship means performance bonuses, commercials, and product endorsements. Stu is now with Huffy. Greg is the owner of GHP BMX and captain of the Cycle Pro GHP team.

Jason Jensen has turned his championship skill (he's won more than 2,000 trophies) into media gold, with national TV exposure in commercials for Wheaties and Kool-Aid. His good looks have made him a popular choice for autograph seekers.

Freestyler R.L. Osborn of the *BMX Action* team tries a little tabletopping. Sailing and swooping, R.L. is a master of high-air hang time. In tabletopping the object is to get your bike as flat as possible, waiting until the last instant before touching down to straighten out.

High flying, getting mega-air, it's one of the ultimate moments for you and your machine. It's hard to say who gets the bigger thrills, you or the crowd when you're being really radical. Here, Martin Aparijo of the Aparijo-Itson team treats the fans to some awesome free-wheeling.

Dawn to dusk, win or lose, in your neighborhood or on the track, the thrill of riding is the heart of the exciting world of BMX.